Weary Warriors, Fainting Saints

Weary Warriors, Fainting Saints

How You Can Outlast
Every Attack of the Enemy

Joyce Meyer

NEW YORK   BOSTON   NASHVILLE

Unless otherwise indicated, all Scripture quotations, are taken from *The Amplified Bible* (AMP). *The Amplified Bible, Old Testament.* Copyright © 1965, 1987 by The Zondervan Corporation. *The Amplified New Testament*, copyright © 1954, 1958, 1987 by The Lockman Foundation. Used by permission.

Verses marked (TLB) are taken from *The Living Bible* © 1971. Used by permission of Tyndale House Publishers, Inc., Wheaton, Illinois 60189. All rights reserved.

Scripture marked KJV are taken from the *King James Version* of the Bible.

Warner Books Edition
Copyright © 1998 by Joyce Meyer
Life In The Word, Inc.
P.O. Box 655
Fenton, Missouri 63026
All rights reserved.

Warner Faith

Time Warner Book Group
1271 Avenue of the Americas, New York, NY 10020
Visit our Web site at www.twbookmark.com.

The Warner Faith name and logo are registered trademarks of Warner Books.

Printed in the United States of America

First Warner Faith Printing: February 2003
10 9 8 7 6 5 4 3

ISBN: 0-446-69103-8

LCCN: 2002110840

CONTENTS

Introduction:

Strength Is Available

Many people today, including Christians, are experiencing weariness. Some Christians are weary to the point of feeling completely worn out or burned out. It may surprise you to know the Bible tells us this would happen!

In describing the end-times, Daniel chapter 7 speaks of the king who makes *war with the saints* (v. 21):

> *And he shall speak words against the Most High [God] and shall wear out the saints of the Most High... (v. 25).*

The Bible tells us in the end-times Satan will wear out the saints! But it also tells us what happens after that:

And the kingdom and the dominion and the greatness of the kingdom under the whole heavens shall be given to the people of the saints of the Most High... (v. 27).

Even though Satan is releasing an attack of weariness against the saints, Jesus came to give us victory over the attacks of Satan.

...The reason the Son of God was made manifest (visible) was to undo (destroy, loosen, and dissolve) the works the devil [has done].

1 John 3:8

Jesus came *to destroy the works of the devil* (KJV). And even though Satan will try to attack us, for those of us who have received Jesus, *He Who lives in you is greater (mightier) than he* [Satan] *who is in the world* (1 John 4:4).

The Lord tells us in His Word that His strength is available to us.

Isaiah 40:29 tells us the Lord, *...gives power to the faint and weary, and to him who has no might He increases strength [causing it to multiply and making it to abound].* Verse 31 tells us we can *run and not be weary...walk and not faint or become tired.*

God has made strength available to those who believe in His Son, Jesus, and have received Him as their Savior, but Satan doesn't want them to know how to draw on it. He wants to wear them out, then attack them even more.

Remember what Amalek did to you on the way when you had come forth from Egypt, How he did not fear God, but when you were faint and weary he attacked you along the way and cut off all the stragglers at your rear.
Deuteronomy 25:17,18

We can consider Amalek and his attack on the Israelites described in the above Scripture a type and shadow of Satan and the method he is using to try to attack, hinder and stop believers today. (See John 10:10.) When the Israelites were faint and weary, Amalek attacked! Satan tries to wear us down to the point of being faint and weary so that once we are in that position, he can intensify his attack to bring us down!

If you, a Christian, are struggling with being weary and wanting to faint -- if you want to just give up and quit — you can see you aren't alone! Satan is bringing this attack of weariness on the body of Christ to try to keep us from receiving the harvest God has for us.

And God **does** have a harvest for us which He **is** preparing.

After we plant seed in the ground, a great deal goes on under the ground as the root system grows before we see the harvest! Because God's kingdom is based on seed planting and harvest (see Mark 4:26-29), after we plant our seed, God is doing a great deal of work "under the ground," out of our sight, to bring our harvest into the natural, visible world.

This "growing stage" is the point when many Christians become weary and want to faint. When they are doing everything in God they know to do — and are doing it over and over without seeing the results they desire in the natural world — they can become weary in well-doing.

They have planted their seeds in faithfulness and diligence but have lost sight of the way the kingdom of God operates in bringing the manifestation of answers through a harvest.

And let us not lose heart and grow weary and faint in acting nobly and doing right, for in due time and at the appointed season we shall reap, if we do not loosen and relax our courage and faint.
Galatians 6:9

We are in a war of thoughts, where the mind is the battlefield. In this war we use God's Word to take captive every thought Satan wants us to think and believe; then instead, we conform our thoughts to the truth in God's Word.

For the weapons of our warfare are not physical [weapons of flesh and blood], but

they are mighty before God for the overthrow
and destruction of strongholds,
[Inasmuch as we] refute arguments and
theories and reasonings and every proud and
lofty thing that sets itself up against the [true]
knowledge of God; and we lead every thought
and purpose away captive into the obedience
of Christ (the Messiah, the Anointed One).
2 Corinthians 10:4,5

We don't need to be overcome by this attack of weariness on the body of Christ. We don't need to be weary warriors, ready to faint in this war! Jesus has provided a way for us to have strength in the midst of the attack. We can consistently operate in strength and in the power of God.

In this book I share nine truths from the Bible that will help you prevent weariness from coming on you and overtaking you. I believe that once you recognize these truths, you will discover you are no longer struggling as you were, or are as frustrated. You will have a different response to situations. You can live so that God's promises for strength are fulfilled in your life every day!

1

GOD IS NEVER LATE, AND HE USUALLY ISN'T EARLY!

———∿∿∿———

Tired, Busy and Moving Fast

When we ask people how they are these days, usually the answer is, "Tired!" or, "Busy!" When I asked what the lifestyle was like in one city, the answer was, "Fast!"

The word "weary" means "faint,"[1] "worn out,"[2] "1. Tired: fatigued. 2. Exhausted of tolerance or patience."[3] It can also be associated with sickness: "...the common accompaniment of 'sickness'" is "weariness of mind...which not infrequently hinders physical recovery..."[4]

Satan is working hard to wear us out. He wants us to faint, be sick at heart and sick in our body. Many people who have no peace of mind, who live in a state of worry can become physically sick from weariness of mind — just from being worn out in their mind. So many people are worn out today, there are even fatigue diseases such as chronic fatigue syndrome.

"Faint" "denotes (a) 'to loose, release,'... (b) 'to unloose,' as a bow-string, 'to relax....'"[5] People who "faint" feel like giving up. Some Christians decide to quit several times a week, but pick themselves up, deciding, again, to go on with God.

Why would you think that you're going to give up and quit? What else would you do?

What else would we do besides serve God? For most of us, what we were doing before receiving the Lord wasn't working. Why would we want to quit and go back to that?

Once when I was having one of my give-up days, I decided to quit. I had been going around saying, "I'm so tired of this. God, I'm so tired of this." I didn't even know exactly what it was I was so tired of.

Then I changed for a while to saying, "I'm trying so hard, God. I'm trying, but nothing's changing." Finally, I said, "That's it. I just give up, God. I can't do this any more; I quit."

I got really dramatic about it — down on the floor on my knees, like in one of those old movies, crying, "Help me, God. Nobody loves me. And I'm trying so hard. I give up — I just quit."

And this is what I heard the Holy Spirit inside me say to me in response — He said, "Really? Really?" Then He began teaching me something very important.

A Good Type of Quitting

The only time the Holy Spirit gets to do anything for us is when we quit trying to do something in our own works long enough to let Him work. I had actually come to a type of believing. I had reached the end of my rope and was expressing my total dependence on the Lord.

I was saying:

"I can't do anything without you, Lord. I can't change myself, my husband or my kids. I can't make prosperity come to me or force a healing on my body. I can't make my ministry grow. I can't force myself to be nice. I've tried to be quiet. Every time instead I talk more than I ever have in my life. I've tried to think positive thoughts, and I have two negative thoughts instead of one."

In the midst of all our human trying, we forget to believe. We often tell God how hard we're trying when the Bible tells us if we will just believe God, He will give us His rest. (Hebrews 3:18,19; 4:9-11.)

The Bible doesn't tell us to try to do everything on our own; it tells us to believe. And it tells us to wait on the Lord.

Have you not known? Have you not heard? The everlasting God, the Lord, the Creator of the ends of the earth, does not faint or grow weary; there is no searching of His understanding. He gives power to the faint and weary, and to him who has no might He increases strength [causing it to multiply and making it to abound].

Even youths shall faint and be weary, and [selected] young men shall feebly stumble and fall exhausted;

But those who wait for the Lord [who expect, look for, and hope in Him] shall change and renew their strength and power; they shall lift *their wings and mount up [close to God] as eagles [mount up to the sun];* ***they shall run***

and not be weary, they shall walk and not
faint or become tired. (Emphasis mine.)
Isaiah 40:28-31

Waiting for the Lord Renews Our Strength

The first reason people can grow weary and faint is from functioning in their own strength rather than waiting on the Lord to renew their strength. The Bible plainly tells us if we don't spend time waiting on the Lord, we will faint. He wants us to stay in Him so that we can run and not get weary, walk and not faint. He wants us to do everything He tells us to do and still have energy.

Waiting on the Lord is an inner heart attitude we develop of, "God, I cannot do anything apart from You." This attitude says, "I'm waiting on You, Lord, all day long. I'm looking to you for what I need: for the wisdom, strength, energy I need and for the anointing to be released through me."

Don't ever think because you have done something well in the past that you can do it well again. Without dependence on God, you can fall flat on your face at any time.

Anointing increases from waiting, depending and leaning on God like a helpless child, saying, "God help me. I need You; I can't do this without You." Until we learn this dependency on God for help and direction, we will be worn out all the time — **weary warriors and fainting saints.**

God's flow of energy will not freely come to us until we understand that the humble are the ones who receive help. *Humble yourselves therefore under the mighty hand of God, that he may exalt you in **due time*** (1 Peter 5:6 KJV). (Emphasis mine.)

Wait On the Lord for the Due Season

The *King James Version* of Galatians 6:9 says, *And let us not be weary in well doing: for in due season we shall reap, if we faint not.*

The Lord promises to bring the harvest, the answers we are waiting for, in due season. Because we don't know exactly when due season will be, many believers grow weary during the wait! They think, "Did I miss my appointment?" The Bible promises that God will never be late, but it doesn't tell us that He usually is early either!

Many times He is the God of the midnight hour. He **is stretching our faith** and teaching us to believe Him for greater things. Believing brings us right into the middle of God's rest. And during the wait our strength is renewed if we wait in faith instead of fear and frustration.

The type of believing that brings us rest when we are waiting for the Lord is this:

"God, I believe You are smarter than I am and that You have a better plan than I do! I believe Your timing and Your ways are better than mine because Your thoughts are above my thoughts." (Isaiah 55:9.)

We must realize that God's timing is more accurate than ours will ever be. This will free us to abandon ourselves to God and say, "Lord, I would like to see the circumstances happening this way, but that doesn't seem to be happening. I'm not going to live my life in frustration from struggling to try to do something about something I can't do anything about or trying to make something happen that I'm obviously not making happen.

"I surrender. I give my idea, my timing, my wants and desires to You. Do what You want to do, the way You want, when You want. And I'm going to rest!"

"Fainthearted" means "small-souled."[6] Because the soul is often defined as the mind, will and emotions, someone who is fainthearted can't mentally handle very much of a problem or challenge coming against them without caving in, wanting to quit and giving up. It isn't very long before they become discouraged, depressed and negative.

When we wait on the Lord and He renews our strength, we become the kind of people the devil can't wear out. We can outlast the devil's attacks, standing against them until we receive the manifestation of our victory in due season.

John 11 gives the account of Jesus raising Lazarus from the dead.

Jesus said, Take away the stone. Martha, the sister of the dead man, exclaimed, But Lord, by this time he [is decaying and] throws off an

offensive odor, for he has been dead four days!
Jesus said to her, Did I not tell you and
promise you that if you would believe and rely
on Me, you would see the glory of God?
                                    John 11:39,40

If there are circumstances in your life
that have been dead for so long they
smell bad, take a simple, childlike stand
and believe: "I don't know what God will
do, but I believe He will do something."

Take Off the Grave Clothes

So they took away the stone. And Jesus lifted
up His eyes and said, Father, I thank You that
You have heard Me.
Yes, I know You always hear and listen to Me,
but I have said this on account of and for the
benefit of the people standing around, so that
they may believe that You did send Me [that
You have made Me Your Messenger].

When He had said this, He shouted with a
loud voice, Lazarus, come out!
And out walked the man who had been dead,
his hands and feet wrapped in burial cloths
(linen strips), and with a [burial] napkin
bound around his face. Jesus said to them, Free
him of the burial wrappings and let him go.
John 11:41-44

In His prayer, Jesus thanked God that He always heard and listened to Him, a simple confident prayer. When we pray, we can always know God is hearing us.

After praying, Jesus called out in a loud voice and commanded Lazarus to come forth from the tomb. When Lazarus came out of the tomb, he was still bound up. Jesus ordered that his grave clothes be removed from him and that he be set free. Many people who are born again are still bound up in grave clothes from the past.

No matter how long we have been in dead circumstances, when Jesus rolls away the stone and says, "Come out," that's a brand new beginning. The Lord wants us to cast off our grave clothes and come out of our tomb, free from the restraints of the past and anything else that drains our strength like worry, fear, negativism, etc.

Instead of meditating on our problems, we can keep our minds and hearts focused on the Lord, trusting ourselves and our situation to God, in simple, childlike faith, waiting patiently for Him to act. If we will do that, He has promised we will witness the mighty manifestation of His glory — in due time, at the appointed season.

2

RECEIVE GOD'S GRACE,
HIS POWER, FOR TODAY

*...do not worry or be anxious about tomorrow,
for tomorrow will have worries and anxieties of
its own. Sufficient for each day is its own trouble.*

Matthew 6:34

God gives us enough grace for one day at a time. And to avoid fatigue and burnout, weariness and fainting, we must learn to live one day at a time.

That's why we are told by Jesus in the above passage to meet each day's challenges as they come and not to borrow trouble from tomorrow. If we will do that, at the appointed time God's grace will be available to us in sufficient supply to help us face and overcome whatever may lie in our path.

Grace

But He gives us more and more grace (power of the Holy Spirit, to meet this evil tendency and all others fully). That is why He says, God sets Himself against the proud and haughty, but gives grace [continually] to the lowly (those who are humble enough to receive it).
James 4:6

Grace is God's unmerited favor. It is the power of the Holy Spirit to help us do whatever we need to do. It is God helping us when we don't deserve His help.

According to James, every day God's grace is poured out upon us to help us resist our evil tendencies. That means that if you and I lean on the Lord, He will give us the grace and power to walk in the fruit of the Spirit, which includes love, joy, peace, patience, kindness, goodness, faithfulness, gentleness, and self-control. (Galatians 5:22,23.)

But we must believe for that grace each day, because it cannot be stored up.

Grace Cannot Be Stored Up

When the Israelites saw it, they said one to another, Manna [What is it?]. For they did not know what it was. And Moses said to them, This is the bread which the Lord has given you to eat.
This is what the Lord has commanded: Let every man gather of it as much as he will need, an omer for each person, according to

*the number of your persons; take it, every man
for those in his tent.
The [people] did so, and gathered, some more,
some less.
When they measured it with an omer, he who
gathered much had nothing over, and he who
gathered little had no lack; each gathered
according to his need.
Moses said, Let none of it be left until morning.*
Exodus 16:15-19

So often we want to try to store up God's grace so that we are covered not only for today but also for tomorrow and all the days ahead. But like the manna that God provided for the Children of Israel, grace doesn't work that way.

Do you know why grace can't be stored up? Because it doesn't take any trust to live that way.

When God provided manna for the Israelites, they were told to gather each morning only what they needed for that one day. That was God's way of teaching them that they were to live by faith, believing that each day what they needed for that day would be supplied.

That was true for every day except the Sabbath. They had to gather twice as much on the day before the Sabbath so they would not have to work on the day of rest. What they gathered the day before would keep through the Sabbath. But if they tried to gather more than they needed on any other day, it would rot and stink.

When you and I start worrying and fretting about what we are going to do tomorrow, or any other time down the road, we are trying to gather manna for the future, and it won't work.

God wants us to trust Him for our daily existence, as we see in Matthew 6:11 in which Jesus taught us to pray: *Give us this day our daily bread.* Note that the Lord did not teach us to pray, "Give us today the bread we will need for tomorrow," but rather, "Give us this day our bread for today."

God wants us to believe that when the time comes, what we need will be there. He wants us to believe and enter His rest.

I realize that some of us have some real questions about our future. Some of us may be facing some pretty frightening and confusing times. Some may have heard that they will be losing their job, and they are naturally concerned about what will happen to them and their families.

If you are caught in a situation like that, and you are concerned about what the future holds for you and your loved ones, the first thing you must do is make a decision not to worry. Believe God will show you what to do when the time comes.

One reason you should do that is because what you fear may never happen.

Fear Not

Are not two little sparrows sold for a penny?
And yet not one of them will fall to the ground
without your Father's leave (consent) and notice.
But even the very hairs of your head are
all numbered.

*Fear not, then; you are of more value than
many sparrows.*

Matthew 10:29-31

Do you know what the word "fear"
means? I like to spell it this way: *F-E-A-R*,
which stands for "False Evidence Appear-
ing Real."

So often Satan tries to lie to us and
make us think that something awful is
going to happen to us. Usually it ends up
not happening that way at all. So we fuss
and fret and worry for nothing.

Trusting God is the only thing that
brings real rest.

That's why I highly recommend that
you not spend much time today thinking
about tomorrow — except to make
whatever plans you need to make to

handle what you know for sure is going to take place.

When I travel I make plans and schedules and itineraries ahead of time. I know I want to be in a certain city and registered into a particular hotel on a definite day at a specific hour so I will be sure to get enough sleep the night before to be rested and refreshed for the next day's meeting.

Then when I get ready to head back home, I plan ahead of time so I will be sure to make the connections I need to make to arrive there on time.

Once I get back I have a schedule of activities all laid out. I know I have a board meeting on Monday, for example, and a television program on Tuesday, and so on.

So I am not saying that you and I should not think about the future at all or that we should not make plans and provision for it. That would be foolish.

I am saying that we should not become so concerned and anxious and nervous about all these things that we get worn out trying to keep up an impossible schedule and pace.

From my own experience in life, I have learned that if I get overloaded despite all my best-laid plans and programs, at just the right moment God will send someone to help, or something else will happen, so that everything works out for the best. There are things in life I cannot foresee or plan or prepare for. I can only trust Him to provide what is needed, when the need arises.

Grace for the Occasion

One time an old saint and a younger believer were being held together in prison awaiting their execution the next day when they would be burned at the stake.

As the younger man struck a match to light a candle, he burned his finger. Yelling in pain, he began to weep in agony and doubt, saying, "If it hurts this much now to burn my finger, how can I possibly stand to be burned at the stake tomorrow?"

The old saint, filled with the wisdom of God, answered, "Son, God didn't ask you to burn your finger, but He is asking you to die for His glory. In the morning when it is time for you to face the fire, His grace will be there to see you through that test."

That is a lesson each of us needs to learn. You and I may not feel at all capable of handling what lies ahead. We may think we do not have the courage and wisdom and strength to live each day as it comes. We may pray for God to deliver us. But often the Lord leaves us that way on purpose, so we will have to trust Him and not ourselves.

One Day at a Time

Sometimes just before a meeting or convention, people will ask me, "Are you ready?"

My answer is usually, "Yes and no."

What I mean is, "No, I'm not ready, but yes, I'm sure God is. I've done my part. I've studied, prayed, and prepared myself to walk out on that platform and watch as God does something through me, as He has done so many times in the past. But no, of myself I don't feel capable of doing this at all."

I don't know how many times I have stood behind a pulpit without the slightest idea what I was going to say. But then it would be just as though a mantle fell upon me. I would know that it was the anointing of God, the power of the Holy Spirit, that had suddenly come upon me. I would hear myself saying things I had not planned on saying at all.

I have even preached entire sermons on subjects I had not prepared at all.

But God knew what I needed, and He provided it.

That is the way you and I must learn to live — one day at a time. If we don't, we are going to end up as **weary warriors and fainting saints.**

Avoid Regret and Dread

God has promised to give us what we need for today. He provides manna only for one day at a time. That's when life starts getting sweet — when it is lived one day at a time.

Most of us have all we can handle in one day anyway. We don't really need to go borrowing trouble from yesterday or tomorrow.

It is all we can do to live today without taking on regret from the past or dread of the future. If we try to do more than that, we are setting ourselves up for weariness and fainting.

Enter the Rest, Cease From Weariness

So then, there is still awaiting a full and complete Sabbath-rest reserved for the [true] people of God;
For he who has once entered [God's] rest also has ceased from [the weariness and pain] of human labors, just as God rested from those labors peculiarly His own.

Hebrews 4:9,10

I believe that weariness is a curse.

As sons and daughters of God, you and I are not supposed to be under the curse, as we see in Galatians 3:13: *Christ purchased our freedom [redeeming us] from the curse (doom) of the Law [and its condemnation] by [Himself] becoming a curse for us, for it is written [in the Scriptures], Cursed is everyone who hangs on a tree (is crucified).*

That means that we are not supposed to be full of weariness. Instead, according to Ephesians 6:10 KJV we are supposed to *...be strong in the Lord, and in the power of his might.* We are supposed to have the strength and energy to do whatever we need to do in our daily lives.

That is part of our heritage as the true people of God, part of the blessing we receive by entering into God's rest.

Don't Become Wearied Out Through Fear

*Therefore, since we do hold and engage in this ministry by the mercy of God [granting us favor, benefits, opportunities, and especially salvation], we do not get discouraged (spiritless and despondent with fear) or become **faint with weariness and exhaustion** (emphasis mine)....*

Therefore we do not become discouraged (utterly spiritless, exhausted, and wearied out through fear). Though our outer man is [progressively] decaying and wasting away, yet our inner self is being [progressively] renewed day after day.

2 Corinthians 4:1,16

In this passage the apostle Paul tells us that we are not to become wearied out through fear.

Do you realize that fear will wear you out? It will also burn you out. It will make you afraid of everything so that you are no good to yourself, to your family, to others, or to the Kingdom of God.

But 1 John 4:18 KJV tells us that perfect love casts out fear. Therefore, if you trust yourself to the love, mercy, and grace of the Lord, you will not become wearied out though fear. His love, mercy, and grace will keep you strong.

One of the primary reasons people become weary and faint is because they exhaust themselves trying to do everything in their own strength and power rather than depending upon the presence and power of the indwelling Holy Spirit.

3
BE WELL BALANCED

—◦◦◦—

Be well balanced (temperate, sober of mind),
be vigilant and cautious at all times; for that
enemy of yours, the devil, roams around like a
lion roaring [in fierce hunger], seeking
someone to seize upon and devour.

1 Peter 5:8

So many of us are tired and worn out today simply because we are out of balance.

The Lord did not create us to go through life dragging our bodies around, feeling like we are going to fall apart. But thank God, there is something we can do to change that situation.

In His Word, God teaches us principles of wisdom, and we have to learn those principles and follow them if we are to see our lives begin to change and become what He intends them to be.

"Marginless Living"

One of the main causes of weariness and fainting, of physical, mental, and spiritual burnout and exhaustion, is what I call "marginless living."

If you have ever taken a class in typing, you know that one of the first things you have to do before typing a page is set the margins on either side. If you don't do that, you will soon be typing off the edge.

That is exactly what many people do with their lives — they fail to set proper margins, or boundaries, so they end up going "off the edge."

The reason we have to have proper margins or boundaries is because the flesh always tends toward excess.

For example, if we listened to our body and did exactly what it wanted to do, most of us would become lazy and just sit around on the couch, watching television and eating everything in sight.

Others of us might go to the other extreme and become such workaholics that the only time we would ever feel good about ourselves would be when we were doing something "constructive" or "productive."

Often marginless people will either become such spendthrifts they buy everything they see, or else become so miserly they try to hoard every penny they get their hands on.

The Bible teaches that we are to be temperate and well balanced. That means we are to avoid extremes of all kinds.

Being temperate and well balanced applies to every aspect of our lives. For example, we are to maintain a balanced diet including all the major food groups in the right proportion. We are to drink the right amount and kinds of fluids, engage in the right amount of physical exercise, and get the proper amount of sleep and rest.

What happens when we get out of balance in any one of these areas?

Sooner or later our body begins to suffer, and we end up weak or sick or worse.

The same is true in our mental, emotional, and spiritual lives.

Don't Go Overboard!

In the spiritual area, imagine for example a young wife and mother who gets born again and baptized in the Holy Spirit. She is so enthusiastic about her new faith that she immediately begins attending several evening Bible classes and early morning prayer meetings each week. She spends every waking moment in prayer, Bible reading or in some kind of spiritual seminar or teaching meeting.

What will likely happen? Obviously it won't be long before her family will begin to suffer. Her husband and children may start to feel neglected and that she is no longer meeting their needs.

What's the problem? It is not that she is too spiritual. It is simply that she has gotten out of balance in that one area. As a wife and mother, she needs to keep her spiritual life in proper balance with the other aspects of her life. If she doesn't, she will end up in trouble.

I like to point out that when the Lord called me to the ministry, I was making up the bed. I think that's important, because a lot of people are out trying to make a ministry who ought to be home making their bed.

If you think you might be called to go into the ministry, be sure your priorities are straight. Get your own house (your own life) in order first before you start going out to set other people's house (their life) in order.

Yes, of course it is good to study the Word of God, attend Bible studies and go to prayer meetings and seminars. But if you become excessive about it, you will get unbalanced. In that case, you will need to cut back on those worthwhile activities and spend more time tending to the other important aspects of your life.

Some people are constantly asking God for more things when they are not taking proper care of what He has already given them. We should not pray and ask God for a bigger house unless the one we have is well cared for.

Laziness and neglect are signs of a lack of balance, of excess in one way. But it is also possible to be excessive the other way.

In my own case, I was a perfectionist. I cleaned my whole house from top to bottom every single day. I vacuumed the carpets, buffed the hardwood floors, cleaned the bathrooms, shined all the mirrors in the house, and polished the furniture. I was so caught up in my **work,** I never had time to do anything but — work, work, work. I was totally out of balance.

If you and I do not lead balanced lives we will open the door to the enemy to come in and cause trouble. That's why we need margins, boundaries, and guidelines for our daily life to keep us from going overboard in one direction or the other.

Tend to Your Own Affairs First

But the man from whom the demons had gone out kept begging and praying that he might accompany Him and be with Him, but [Jesus] sent him away, saying,
Return to your home, and recount [the story] of how many and great things God has done for you. And [the man] departed, proclaiming throughout the whole city how much Jesus had done for him.

Luke 8:38,39

In this story we read how Jesus healed a man by casting the demons out of him. Immediately the man wanted to go with Jesus and spend his whole life as a part of His ministry. But Jesus said no.

Instead, He sent him back home to tend to his own affairs and spread the Good News to his own people.

That is an indication that we are not called to get involved in every good work that may come our way. We don't always need to go out and minister — often we should go home and minister.

We often create our own problems and produce bad fruit simply because we don't know how to say no to anything. We want to be in on everything that is going on.

But the Lord wants us to tend to our own affairs first. If He wants us for a particular ministry, He will speak to us where we are about what He has in mind for us. We should seek to be discerning so we can choose the best over the good.

Choose the Best Over the Good

And this I pray: that your love may abound yet more and more and extend to its fullest development in knowledge and all keen insight [that your love may display itself in greater depth of acquaintance and more comprehensive discernment],
So that you may surely learn to sense what is vital, and approve and prize what is excellent and of real value [recognizing the highest and the best, and distinguishing the moral differences], and that you may be untainted and pure and unerring and blameless [so that with hearts sincere and certain and unsullied, you may approach] the day of Christ [not stumbling nor causing others to stumble].
Philippians 1:9,10

Here in his prayer for the church in Philippi, the apostle Paul prayed that they would understand the difference between what is good and what is excellent.

Many times good is actually the enemy of the best.

We may ask, "Why would God not want me to do this? It's such a good thing." The problem may be that even though it is good, it is not God's best for us. If we insist on doing it anyway, we will be in disobedience. So the good thing turns out to be a bad thing because it leads us away from the perfect will of God.

If you feel you are in danger of becoming unbalanced, **learn to say no.** Trim your life. Prune it back. Consider the things you are currently involved in and decide whether they are the things God has really told you to do.

Remember, God is not obligated to anoint you for anything He has not called you to do. He may have called you to it at one time, but now that call may be fulfilled. Once God's anointing is lifted from something, it is finished. That's when you need to let go of it and move on in obedience to the Lord.

You and I must learn to discern God's best and flow with His anointing. We must learn when God wants us to get involved in something, when He has finished with that job, and when He wants us to move on to something else. We must not allow other people to influence us to become (or remain) involved in something for which we are not chosen and anointed. If we do, we will find ourselves suffering weariness and beginning to faint. **God will not strengthen us to be out of His will.**

Consider the Field

A capable, intelligent, and virtuous woman — who is he who can find her? She is far more precious than jewels and her value is far above rubies or pearls....

She considers a [new] field before she buys or accepts it [expanding prudently and not courting neglect of her present duties by assuming other duties]; with her savings [of time and strength] she plants fruitful vines in her vineyard.

Proverbs 31:10,16

In this passage the writer of Proverbs is speaking of the virtuous woman, but his words apply equally as well to the virtuous man.

One of the virtues of this woman is that she gives thoughtful consideration to her decisions and limits her involvements so she does not become overburdened with responsibilities.

One reason many people are so worn out is simply because they are always saying yes to things God has not told them to do. They get themselves over-booked with something to do every night and day of the week. As a result, they end up frustrated and fatigued. Such people need to learn to be more selective in their commitments.

Life is a series of choices. All of us must learn to make wise choices. We need to do what the virtuous woman of Proverbs 31 does: **think seriously and prudently about expansion before committing ourselves to it.** Luke 14:28 tells us to calculate the cost before starting to build; otherwise, we may not have what is required to finish the project.

We can get into trouble in this area if we react emotionally rather than intelligently. I know because I used to do that all the time. I used to wear myself out trying to do too much. Finally the Lord spoke to me loud and clear: "Joyce, if you want to do what I have called you to do, then you have got to center your life on that one thing."

That was hard on my flesh because I was an "involvee." Because of my nature and personality type, I wanted to be part of everything that was going on. You may be the same way. But that is not God's will for us.

It takes real discipline and obedience to say no to something we want to say yes to. But that is what we must do. When offered something we know in our heart is not God's best for us, we must simply say, "No, I can't do that. I already have enough to do, and I am not going to commit to anything else, because if I do it will cause me to be overloaded." **People who want to be a success must stay focused.**

Realistic or Idealistic?

I have strength for all things in Christ Who empowers me [I am ready for anything and equal to anything through Him Who infuses inner strength into me; I am self-sufficient in Christ's sufficiency].

Philippians 4:13

This verse is often quoted as proof that with the power of God in us we are able to, as the *King James Version* says, *do all things.*

Yet *The Living Bible* translation of this verse may come closer to its real meaning: *for I can do everything God asks me to with the help of Christ who gives me the strength and power.*

As I have said, God is under no obligation to anoint with His strength and power anything He has not told us to do. If we go ahead and act on what we want or decide to do, no matter how good the work may be, we are operating in our own strength and power. Sooner or later it will fail us and leave us weary and fainting.

We must learn to be realistic, not idealistic. Idealism says, "I can do it all!" Realism says, "I can do everything God asks me to do." That is an important difference — one that requires real spiritual wisdom and discernment.

When faced with a decision about some new opportunity or challenge, we need to stop and ask ourselves some serious questions: "Do I really want to do this? Do I realistically have the time and energy to carry it through? Am I willing to make the commitment and sacrifices it will take to do it the way it needs to be done? Am I acting in response to the revealed will of God for me, or am I acting in response to my own emotionalism?"

It is easy to get carried away with emotion rather than using wise judgment. Certain personality types are more susceptible to that kind of enticement than others. There are some of us who naturally get all enthusiastic about anything new and exciting. But that is being idealistic, not realistic.

I have a name for people who allow themselves to be carried away with emotion; I call them "spiritual surfers." They are the ones who are always ready and waiting to jump on the next "wave" to come along. Such people think if there is not something exciting happening in their lives all the time, they are not in the will of God. As soon as the newness wears off or the excitement dies down in one place, they run some place else looking for "the move of the Spirit." They forget that much of life is, as one young man told me he had learned, "just getting up and going to bed, getting up and going to bed."

Martha or Mary?

But Martha [overly occupied and too busy] was distracted with much serving; and she came up to Him and said, Lord, is it nothing to You that my sister has left me to serve alone? Tell her then to help me [to lend a hand and do her part along with me]!

But the Lord replied to her by saying, Martha,
Martha, you are anxious and troubled about
many things;
There is need of only one or but a few things.
Mary has chosen the good portion [that which
is to her advantage], which shall not be taken
away from her.

Luke 10:40-42

Do you know why some people are late everywhere they go? It's because they are Marthas rather than Marys. That is, they are simply trying to do too much.

They have so many things on their agenda when they leave the house in the morning they have to rush through traffic to get to their first obligation. They have their day's itinerary timed down to the last second and are counting on hitting every green light so nothing will keep them from arriving on time.

When they get out on the street, some sweet little old man trying to get to the grocery store to buy himself a carton of milk gets in the way and holds up the line of traffic by driving at a snail's pace.

These born-again, Spirit-filled people end up ranting and raving at the poor little old man because he is keeping them from barreling through life to do all their "good works"!

When they do finally get to their destination, they are in such a stew they go through their entire day hurried and harried. Then they wonder why they come home at night worn to a frazzle with their nerves on edge. They work and worry through the evening and fall into bed at a late hour and sleep fitfully because of all that is going on in their mind and heart. Then they get up the next day and start the process all over again.

Does that describe your life? Do you go through your day grouchy and grumpy, fuming and complaining because you have so many things to do you aren't getting the rest and relaxation you need to feel and do your best? Are you complaining about your schedule yet failing to realize you are the one who made it?

Are you sick and tired of being sick and tired? If so, then perhaps you need to make some changes in your life. The first change is the decision to be realistic rather than idealistic, to limit your commitments to what you are truly able to handle through the indwelling power of God.

Don't Be Rash

It is a snare to a man to utter a vow [of consecration] rashly and [not until] afterward inquire [whether he can fulfill it].
Proverbs 20:25

In this verse the writer of Proverbs tells us that it is a trap for us to commit ourselves to something before we have determined whether we can fulfill it or not.

When we are asked to get involved in some work, we need to respond, "Let me think about it."

In my own life, I have learned there are times to hold off making a decision —

sometimes even buying a dress on sale — until I can get away and consider the situation from all angles. I am aware that I need to avoid making snap decisions that I may regret later.

All of us need to stop living by our emotions. Instead, we need to be careful to look for God's anointing. One way we can discern that anointing is by following that which gives us a sense of inner peace.

Let Peace Rule

And let the peace (soul harmony which comes) from Christ rule (act as umpire continually) in your hearts [deciding and settling with finality all questions that arise in your minds, in that peaceful state] to which as [members of Christ's] one body you were also called [to live]. And be thankful (appreciative), [giving praise to God always].

Colossians 3:15

In your quest to avoid or overcome weariness and fainting, be led by peace and wisdom.

Learn to use discernment in your life.

Don't be pushed or pressured into doing what everybody else is doing. Take your time and think things through, deciding what is best for you.

Don't commit yourself to anything until you know you are realistically able to see it through and complete it.

Be a person of commitment and integrity. If you say you are going to do something, then do it.

If you will use wisdom and discretion, you will be guided and directed so that your every decision will bring you closer to the blessed peace and rest that come with walking in the Spirit rather than by the flesh.

4
SIMPLIFY YOUR LIFE

———

You were wearied with the length of your way
[in trying to find rest and satisfaction in
alliances apart from the true God], yet you
did not say, There is no result or profit....
Isaiah 57:10

There is such a lack of simplicity in our society today, even among God's people.

One reason so many Christians today are worn out and faint is because their lives are complicated. Complication drains energy and produces frustration and fatigue which lead to all kinds of problems.

One translation of the first line of this verse from Isaiah says, "You are wearied out through the multiplicity of your ways." **The answer for the problem of multiplicity is a return to simplicity.**

Increase Brings Complication

When goods increase, they who eat them increase also. And what gain is there to their owner except to see them with his eyes?
The sleep of a laboring man is sweet, whether he eats little or much, but the fullness of the rich will not let him sleep.
Ecclesiastes 5:11,12

In our modern acquisitive society, we seem to have the idea that more is always better. But the writer of Ecclesiastes warns us that the more our goods increase, the more complicated our lives become.

I once heard a pastor say, "I have so many suits in my closet I get worn out trying to decide which one to wear."

Then he went onto explain.

"When I was just starting out in the ministry I only had two suits, one was blue and the other was black. One day I would wear the blue one and the next day I would wear the black one.

"Now that I have become prosperous, it is a lot harder and more complicated to get dressed in the morning because I have so many choices to make."

That does not mean that God does not want us to prosper, but that we must maintain a proper balance in every area of our existence.

If we are not careful even our affluence can cause us some very real problems. I recommend "pruning your possessions."

Sharing Simplifies

...He who has two tunics..., let him share with him who has none; and he who has food, let him do it the same way.
Luke 3:11

If God is blessing us, we need to go through our homes, closets and pantries and prune them on a regular basis. We need to take out a lot of the excess and share them with those to whom they would be a real blessing. When my house starts looking cluttered with *things,* I start looking for *things* to give away.

In Romans 12:8, we are told, ...*he who contributes, let him do it in simplicity and liberality....*

If we will do that, if we will give in simplicity and liberality, we can assure that not only will the lives of others be blessed, but also that our own life will not become so encumbered with possessions it gets complicated.

Keep It Simple

But I fear, lest by any means, as the serpent beguiled Eve through his subtilty, so your minds should be corrupted from the simplicity that is in Christ.

2 Corinthians 11:3 KJV

Because I tend toward being a complicated person, I have noticed that complicated people like me are easily burned out. The reason is because we make everything so much harder than it ought to be.

Let me give you an example.

One night my husband Dave and I had an argument. After it was over, we more or less made up with one another.

Being a person who is not easily bothered or upset and who does not carry a grudge, Dave thought the whole thing was settled and forgotten. So he went on to bed and quickly fell sound asleep.

But I was still mad. I was upset because I didn't understand how two grown up intelligent human beings could start out having a conversation about one thing like their children and wind up in a fight over something that had happened ten years earlier.

So I went into my home office and vowed, "I'm going to figure out why this kind of thing happens between us if I have to stay up all night long! I'm missing something here, so what is it?"

So while I was in my office studying and stewing, Dave was in the bed snuggling and snoring.

All the time I knew I was going to be totally exhausted the next day, which meant I would be a classic grouch and hard to get along with. Still I went right on asking, "What am I going to do about this situation? What am I going to do?"

I was desperately trying to figure out some way to ensure that Dave and I would never have that problem again. I analyzed what I said and what he said and what I did and what he did. On and on it went until finally I said out loud, "God, what am I going to do?"

Just then the Lord spoke to me and answered, **"Why don't you try going to bed and getting some sleep?"**

At the time I found that extremely difficult to do. I was so complicated it was hard for me to accept the simplicity that is ours in Christ Jesus.

Is your life complicated? If so, maybe you need to do what I had to learn to do: **simplify, simplify, simplify.**

Do Not Frustrate God's Grace

I do not frustrate the grace of God....
Galatians 2:21 KJV

When I was going through that troubling time in my life, the Lord had to break a lot of fleshly nonsense off of me. He had to deal with me about many things. One of them was frustration.

Any time we feel frustrated it is because we are not receiving God's grace. We are trying to do things on our own. We are not leaning on the Lord, trusting Him to see us through.

Instead, we are trying to get rid of something we don't want, or else we are trying to get something we do want and cannot figure out how to get it.

For example, in my own life I became totally frustrated trying to make myself into a holy person. I was trying to produce the fruit of the Spirit on my own. I had not yet learned that if I would become rooted and grounded in Christ, He would produce the fruit in and through me.

Abide in Me and Bear Much Fruit

Dwell in Me, and I will dwell in you. [Live in Me, and I will live in you.] Just as no branch can bear fruit of itself without abiding in (being vitally united to) the vine, neither can you bear fruit unless you abide in Me.
I am the Vine; you are the branches. Whoever lives in Me and I in him bears much (abundant) fruit. However, apart from Me [cut off from vital union with Me] you can do nothing.
John 15:4,5

I had not yet learned what abiding in Jesus meant. Nor did I understand what He was talking about in verse 7 when He said, *If you live in Me [abide vitally united to Me] and My words remain in you and continue to live in your hearts, ask whatever you will, and it shall be done for you.*

The reason I did not fully understand these things is because I was still being cleansed and pruned, as we read in verse 3: *You are cleansed and pruned already, because of the word which I have given you [the teachings I have discussed with you].*

What the Lord was teaching me is that if I would cease all my struggling and doing and simply abide in Him, He would abide in me. I would then bear much fruit, and He would continue to cleanse and prune me so I would bear even more, richer, and more excellent fruit.

That means that you and I cannot expect to do things on our own and find any measure of lasting success or rest and peace. Rather than being blessed, we will be cursed.

The Curse of Complication

Thus says the Lord: Cursed [with great evil] is the strong man who trusts in and relies on frail man, making weak [human] flesh his arm, and whose mind and heart turn aside from the Lord.
For he shall be like a shrub or a person naked and destitute in the desert; and he shall not see any good come, but shall dwell in the parched places in the wilderness, in an uninhabited salt land.

Jeremiah 17:5,6

This sounds like a lot of people I know. It also sounds like the way I used to be: dry, burned out, worn out, fainting for lack of spiritual water.

The reason I was in that cursed condition is because I was depending on the arm of flesh — my own strength and knowledge and ability — rather than on the arm of the Lord.

God left me in that curse of frustration until I came to see that what I needed was to give up all my complicated planning, figuring, and striving and simply abide in Him, allowing Him to do the work that needed to be done in me and through me.

The Blessing of Simplicity

[Most] blessed is the man who believes in, trusts in, and relies on the Lord, and whose hope and confidence the Lord is. For he shall be like a tree planted by the

*waters that spreads out its roots by the river;
and it shall not see and fear when the heat
comes; but its leaf shall be green. It shall not
be anxious and full of care in the year of
drought, nor shall it cease yielding fruit.*

Jeremiah 17:7,8

Do you realize what the Lord is telling us in this passage? He is saying that the more you and I believe in, trust in, and rely on Him, the more blessed we will be. The more we give up our struggling and striving and simply lean on and depend on Him, the greater will be our reward.

Part of my teaching library is a message titled "Rest and Be Blessed." That is the lesson that each of us needs to learn and be reminded of again and again.

What we are yearning for and looking for is not complicated, it is very simple: *Trust (lean on, rely on, and be confident) in the Lord and do good; so shall you dwell in the land and feed surely on His faithfulness, and truly you shall be fed* (Psalm 37:3).

Keep it simple: trust God.

5

BE PATIENT

—~~—

So be patient, brethren, [as you wait] till the
coming of the Lord. See how the farmer waits
expectantly for the precious harvest from the
land. [See how] he keeps up his patient [vigil]
over it until he receives the early and late rains.
So you also must be patient. Establish your
hearts [strengthen and confirm them in the
final certainty], for the coming of the Lord is
very near.

James 5:7,8

One of the main reasons so many of us
today are weary and fainting is because
we expect instant results from our efforts.

As we saw before, in Galatians 6:9 we
were warned by the apostle Paul not to

allow ourselves to become weary in well doing, because in due season we will reap — if we do not faint and give up.

At Just the Right Moment

Let us then fearlessly and confidently and boldly draw near to the throne of grace (the throne of God's unmerited favor to us sinners), that we may receive mercy [for our failures] and find grace to help in good time for every need [appropriate help and well-timed help, coming just when we need it].
Hebrews 4:16

In His Word the Lord has assured us that we can come boldly before His throne, bringing our needs to Him in complete confidence, knowing that He will act on our behalf and provide exactly what we need at just the right moment.

The lesson we must learn from all this is that believing God places us right in the very center, not of the world's turmoil and confusion, but of God's perfect rest and peace.

Perfect Trust Brings Perfect Peace

Do not fret or have any anxiety about anything, but in every circumstance and in everything, by prayer and petition (definite requests), with thanksgiving, continue to make your wants known to God.
And God's peace [shall be yours, that tranquil state of a soul assured of its salvation through Christ, and so fearing nothing from God and being content with its earthly lot of whatever sort that is, that peace] which transcends all understanding shall garrison and mount guard over your

hearts and minds in Christ Jesus.
Philippians 4:6,7

Believing God should not make us frustrated or joyless. Instead, it should bring us that perfect rest and peace that are to be found only in trusting God with all our heart and mind, as we read in Isaiah 26:3: *You will guard him and keep him in perfect and constant peace whose mind [both its inclination and its character] is stayed on You, because he commits himself to You, leans on You, and hopes confidently in You.*

But in order to enjoy that perfect rest and peace, we must learn to trust not only God's perfect provision but also His perfect timing. We must learn to relax and enjoy the wait as well as the way.

Have a Nice Trip!

My times are in Your hands; deliver me from the hands of my foes and those who pursue me and persecute me.

Psalm 31:15

We must learn to trust God to do whatever He needs to do, the way He needs to do it, when He needs to do it.

For example, if my ministry is not growing as I would like for it to, I have to believe that God has a plan for it and that He will cause it to grow in the way He wants it to grow, when He wants it to do so. There may be something else in my life He needs to do or something else He needs to work out in order to bring to pass His perfect plan.

In the meanwhile, I try to do what I teach others to do: enjoy where I am on the way to where I am going.

Many believers today are going somewhere, but they are not enjoying the trip. Whatever your situation or circumstances may be, don't waste your life trying to get someplace else without enjoying to the fullest where you are at the moment.

Submit your life to God in complete confidence. Trust Him to bring to pass exactly what is needed, at just the right time. In the meanwhile, enjoy the trip — just don't become weary on the way!

Remember that we are to supposed to be going from glory to glory. (2 Corinthians 3:18 KJV.) That means we are to be on the move. We are not to spend our lives waiting for someone else in the Body of Christ to come along and pick us up on the side of the highway of life and take us where we need to be.

There are no hitchhikers on the road to glory!

We must learn to walk in victory every day of our life, confronting and overcoming the enemy who tries to discourage us and wear us out and cause us to give up and quit.

On our way to where the Holy Spirit is leading us, we are going to have to face and overcome many obstacles. But the Lord has told us that we are more than conquerors through the One Who loved us and gave Himself for us. (Romans 8:37.)

What does it mean to be a conqueror? It means to know that we are winners before we ever enter the fight.

There will be things we have to go through, there will be tears to be shed, but if we know how to deal with them, trials and hardships and difficulties only work to our advantage. Why? Because they cause us to press on harder and to draw closer to the Lord, Who is the only One Who can see us through to eventual victory.

Carry Through to Deliverance

Shall I bring to the [moment of] birth and not cause to bring forth? says the Lord. Shall I Who causes to bring forth shut the womb? says your God.

Isaiah 66:9

We forget that we have sown the seed in good ground and that what we have sown in faith God has promised to bring to manifestation and fruition.

Although we may not always be able to see it with our natural eyes, we must believe that God is at work behind the scenes bringing forth the birth — at the time He has set and appointed.

I remember when I was pregnant with each of our children. I carried all of them to term and beyond. One of them was almost six weeks late. I was so worn out with carrying that child I asked the doctor to start my labor.

That is the way you and I become spiritually. We are pregnant with dreams and visions, but we get so tired of waiting for them to manifest we start our own labor.

After one trip to the hospital, my doctor finally told me, "Go home and relax. This baby is not going to come until it is good and ready."

The lesson you and I need to learn from that experience is that we are not to waste our lives trying to make something happen that is not in God's perfect plan and timing. If we keep trying, we will just end up as weary warriors and fainting saints.

That is not God's will for us. He wants us to learn to be patient. He wants us to trust Him to complete and bring forth — on His own schedule — the good work He has begun in us. (Philippians 1:6.)

If good seed has been planted in good soil, sooner or later it will produce good fruit. **Keep on keeping on, and refuse to give up!**

Let Your Life Be a Seed

I assure you, most solemnly I tell you, Unless a grain of wheat falls into the earth and dies, it remains [just one grain; it never becomes more but lives] by itself alone. But if it dies, it produces many others and yields a rich harvest.
John 12:24

Instead of trying to rush things, we need to slow down and spend more time waiting on God in faith and patience. We should concentrate on depositing ourselves with God, trusting Him to take care of us to bring forth what we need day by day as we patiently wait for Him.

6

KEEP YOUR EYES
ON GOD, NOT ON
YOUR PROBLEMS

—⁓—

Why, O Jacob, do you say, and declare, O
Israel, My way and my lot are hidden from the
Lord, and my right is passed over without
regard from my God?
Have you not known? Have you not heard? The
everlasting God, the Lord, the Creator of the
ends of the earth, does not faint or grow weary;
there is no searching of His understanding.

Isaiah 40:27,28

Many times the reason we are so weary
and faint is because we are paying more
attention to our problems than we are to

God. Constantly thinking and talking about problems or concerns magnifies them above the Lord.

I once knew a lady who discovered a mysterious lump on her body. She went around feeling it all the time. She was so focused on it and so concerned about it, she literally wore herself out to the point of becoming sick and faint. Her worry produced symptoms that had nothing to do with the lump.

You and I may do the same thing with something as slight as a fever. We may take our temperature and see that it is a bit high. We may then set in to worry and fret about it until we really do make ourselves ill.

If God doesn't instantly answer our prayers and miraculously take away our sickness, we may conclude He is either unaware of our situation or unwilling to do anything about it.

When we do that, we are doing exactly what the people of Israel were doing in Isaiah 40:27. We are asking ourselves, as they did, "Doesn't God see what is going on in my life? Why doesn't He do something about my terrible situation?"

In verse 28, Isaiah's answer to the people was that God does not faint or get weary, and that there is no searching of His understanding.

In other words he was saying to them, "Quit your whining and complaining! Do you really think for one moment that

God does not know exactly what is happening to you or that He does not have the willingness or the power to do anything about it?"

If we want to lose our peace and joy, here is a marvelous way to do it — by trying to figure out what God is doing or not doing, and why.

We need to give up our excessive questioning and reasoning. We must remember there is no searching of God's understanding. That means we are not going to figure Him out. When He chooses to reveal Himself to us or become involved in our situation, He will. Until that time we are to keep our eyes on Him and not on our negative situation.

Our job is not to understand God but to trust Him and be obedient to Him. That is how we receive from Him the strength and energy we need to keep from becoming weary and faint in the midst of trials and temptations. Remember this: Trust always requires unanswered questions.

The Lord Gives Power

He gives power to the faint and weary, and to him who has no might He increases strength [causing it to multiply and making it to abound].
Isaiah 40:29

When I feel myself starting to get weary and faint, I go to the Lord. I have learned it is better to keep up regular, consistent maintenance than it is to wait until a breakdown occurs and then try to repair the damage.

It is wise not to use up everything we have and totally deplete all our resources — physically, mentally, emotionally, and spiritually.

It is easy to get burned out from just being continually upset and frustrated about problems, especially when we focus on them rather than keeping our eyes on the Lord.

It is possible to burn out mentally and emotionally just by trying to figure out everything instead of trusting ourselves and our situation to God.

It is also possible to wear out physically by working too hard and not eating, sleeping, resting, and relaxing properly.

In fact, it is easy to get weary and faint simply from being too serious minded all the time.

Because I have a tendency to be a worrier and a workaholic, I once received a word from the Lord on this subject. He told me to lighten up and quit taking everything in life so seriously. He told me I needed to learn to enjoy life more.

You and I need to quit relying so much on ourselves and our strengths and abilities. God has promised to provide us the strength and energy and power we need to keep going. We need to quit being so intense about everything in our life. We need to learn to relax more and allow the Lord to restore and renew us before we fall apart completely.

Even Youths Get Weary and Faint

*Even youths shall faint and be weary, and
[selected] young men shall feebly stumble and
fall exhausted;
But those who wait for the Lord [who expect,
look for, and hope in Him] shall change and
renew their strength and power; they shall lift
their wings and mount up [close to God] as
eagles [mount up to the sun]; they shall run
and not be weary, they shall walk and not
faint or become tired.*

Isaiah 40:30,31

This passage is telling us that if we try to do things on our own without God, even if we are young and strong and energetic, we will still fail.

We need to be delivered from the spirit of independence.

Too often we want to ignore God and live our own lives, doing exactly what we want to do, running along in the strength of our own flesh. Then when we get into trouble, we want to call upon the Lord to deliver us and set us back on our feet again so we can once more rush headlong down the paths we have chosen for ourselves.

All the time we are wearing ourselves out because we are trying to make it through this world still wrapped in the burial clothes of our old life and old ways.

Bound Up or Set at Liberty?

...be not grieved and depressed, for the joy of the Lord is your strength and stronghold.
Nehemiah 8:10

Many people are still bound by grave clothes — all of those things that keep us bound up so we are not able to serve the Lord freely and fully. Two of those things are weariness and fainting, which often cause us to go through life without strength, energy, joy, peace, or power.

Some believers are still so wrapped up in their grave clothes they walk around looking like mummies. They are so stiff and hard, they look as though smiling would break their face.

One reason many of us believers go around looking so sad and somber is because we are always meditating on our problems rather than focusing on the promises!

By that I do not mean that we are to go through life swinging from chandeliers and laughing hilariously all the time. But I do believe we are supposed to be the happiest people on the face of the earth.

You and I are not to be filled with hype, but with hope, remembering that the joy of the Lord is our strength. It all depends on where we keep our eyes: on our problems or on the promises.

7

NEVER COMPARE PROBLEMS
OR BLESSINGS

—∾—

*...that enemy of yours, the devil, roams
around like a lion roaring [in fierce hunger],
seeking someone to seize upon and devour.
Withstand him; be firm in faith [against his
onset — rooted, established, strong,
immovable, and determined], knowing that
the same (identical) sufferings are appointed
to your brotherhood (the whole body of
Christians) throughout the world.*

1 Peter 5:8,9

One thing that will definitely wear us
out is comparing our problems with the
problems of others.

If we are not careful, even our suffering can become a source of pride or of resentment.

No matter how badly someone else is suffering we always want to think that we are suffering worse than they are. That will either make us feel superior to them, or it will make us want to question God, as Peter did when He asked Jesus about John.

Let's look at this story to see how it relates to us today.

Do You Love Me?

When they had eaten, Jesus said to Simon Peter, Simon, son of John, do you love Me more than these [others do — with reasoning, intentional, spiritual devotion, as one loves

the Father]? He said to Him, Yes, Lord, You
know that I love You [that I have deep,
instinctive, personal affection for You, as for a
close friend]. He said to Him, Feed My lambs.
Again He said to him the second time, Simon,
son of John, do you love Me [with reasoning,
intentional, spiritual devotion, as one loves
the Father]? He said to Him. Yes, Lord, You
know that I love You [that I have a deep,
instinctive, personal affection for You, as for a
close friend]. He said to him, Shepherd (tend)
My sheep.
He said to him the third time, Simon, son of
John, do you love Me [with a deep, instinctive,
personal affection for Me, as for a close
friend]? Peter was grieved (was saddened and
hurt) that He should ask him the third time,
Do you love Me? And he said to Him, Lord,
You know everything; You know that I love
You [that I have a deep, instinctive, personal

*affection for You, as for a close friend]. Jesus
said to him, Feed My sheep.*
John 21:15-17

Here in this passage Jesus is dealing
with Peter about some hard things he is
going to have to face and go through in
the future.

He begins by taking care of some
unfinished business from the past; namely,
Peter's guilt over his three-time denial of
Him in public just before His crucifixion,
right after boasting that although everyone
else might fail Jesus, he never would!

Let's look at Peter's boast to see the
danger in comparing ourselves with others.

I'll Never Fail!

*Then Jesus said to them, You will all be
offended and stumble and fall away because of*

*Me this night [distrusting and deserting Me],
for it is written, I will strike the Shepherd, and
the sheep of the flock will be scattered.
But after I am raised up [to life again], I will
go ahead of you to Galilee.
Peter declared to Him, Though they all are
offended and stumble and fall away because
of You [and distrust and desert You], I will
never do so.
Jesus said to him, Solemnly I declare to you,
this very night, before a single rooster crows,
you will deny and disown Me three times.
Peter said to Him, Even if I must die with You,
I will not deny or disown You! And all the
disciples said the same thing.*

Matthew 26:31-35

Here we see Peter telling Jesus outright
that He is wrong when He predicts that
all of His disciples are going to distrust
and desert Him.

"Although everyone else may do that, I never will!" boasts impetuous Peter. "I am even willing to die right alongside You!"

Of course, we know that is not what happened. Proud, boastful Peter denied his Lord three times in front of a crowd of witnesses at the very moment when Jesus needed his support the most. When he heard the rooster crow and saw Jesus looking at him, Peter left in tears.

Now Jesus has been raised from the dead and has met with His disciples beside the Sea of Galilee where He has prepared breakfast for all of them. It is after the meal that Jesus turns to Peter privately and begins to question him about his commitment to Him.

No wonder Peter is upset when Jesus keeps asking him if he truly loves Him. It reminds him all too clearly of his public failure and denial. Naturally, he would like to find some way to excuse himself for having been as weak and cowardly as all the others to whom he compared himself so favorably.

But Jesus will have none of that. He knows exactly what Peter is capable of, just as He knows what you and I are capable of.

The encouraging thing is that He does not give up on Peter or on us, despite our human weakness and failure. He gives us a second chance, just as He did Peter. But, as with Peter, it may not be exactly what we expect or desire.

Follow Me!

*I assure you, most solemnly I tell you, when
you were young you girded yourself [put on
your own belt or girdle] and you walked about
wherever you pleased to go. But when you
grow old you will stretch out your hands, and
someone else will put a girdle around you and
carry you where you do not wish to go.
He said this to indicate by what kind of death
Peter would glorify God. And after this, He
said to him, Follow Me!*

John 21:18,19

Here Peter is given his second chance.
Jesus tells him in essence that even
though he has failed miserably, his life
and ministry are not over. Peter still has a
work to do — feeding and caring for
Jesus' flock after He Himself has ascended

into heaven to sit at the right hand of the Father in glory.

But Jesus also warns Peter of what lies ahead for him if he does continue to serve Him. He foretells that one day he will indeed die for Him, just as Peter boasted he would.

Then Jesus challenges Peter and tests His commitment by commanding him — just as He commands you and me today — "Follow Me."

But What About This Man!

But Peter turned and saw the disciple whom Jesus loved, following — the one who also had leaned back on His breast at the supper and had said, Lord, who is it that is going to betray You? When Peter saw him, he said to Jesus, Lord, what about this man?

Jesus said to him, If I want him to stay
(survive, live) till I come, what is that to you?
[What concern is it of yours?] You follow Me!
John 21:20-22

The mistake Peter is making is trying to compare his situation with someone else's. Jesus lets him know right away that is not his concern. His job is simply to be obedient to the Lord and follow Him — whatever the consequences might be.

That is exactly what the Lord is telling you and me today: "Forget about what others are doing or going through. That's none of your business. You follow Me!" **Don't compare your trials or your blessings with the ones other people are experiencing.**

James tells us that everyone is going through trials and tribulations of one kind or another. They may not all be equal, but they all have their consequences. Comparing our problems with those of others is no help to us or them.

If we find someone who has more problems than we do, we may take it as evidence that we are more righteous or more in favor with the Lord than they are.

That was the mistake that both the disciples and the Pharisees made when they judged the blind man whom Jesus healed in John 9:1-41. They assumed that because he was born blind either he or his parents had sinned in some way. Jesus made it clear that was not the case at all.

That's why it is always dangerous to compare problems. We might end up drawing the wrong conclusions about ourselves, about others, and about God.

It is also dangerous to compare blessings. Too often we get to thinking that success is an indication of God's love and favor. If someone has more than we do, we get jealous and envious. We think our pocketbook or bank account or house or ministry has got to be as big as everyone else's. If we are not careful, that kind of thinking will lead us into big trouble.

If we find someone who has more success or possessions or fewer troubles than we do, we may start feeling sorry for ourselves and begin questioning God, wondering what's wrong with us that He isn't blessing us as much as He is them, or why He seems to lay so much more on us than He does on them.

Never make the mistake of comparing either your problems or your blessings with those of other people.

If you refuse to do that but instead determine to follow the Lord whatever the consequences, it will help you to stay strong and not become wearied and faint.

8

Understand God's Way of Dealing

—〰—

For My thoughts are not your thoughts,
neither are your ways My ways, says the Lord.
For as the heavens are higher than the earth,
so are My ways higher than your ways and
My thoughts than your thoughts.

Isaiah 55:8,9

A lack of understanding of how God deals with us will wear us out.

Why?

Because if we don't understand how God deals with us, we will end up fighting and resisting things thinking they are an attack from the devil when in reality they are an attempt by the Lord to do something good in our life.

We know that God does not do bad things. But sometimes what we fail to realize is that everything that feels bad *to* us is not necessarily bad *for* us.

Take, for example, medical practices.

Suppose the doctor discovers a malignant growth in our body. We can ignore it and hope it will go away, or we can elect to undergo treatment or even surgery to remove the growth and destroy the cancer cells to ensure they do not spread to other places of our system.

That procedure may be uncomfortable or even painful, but it is necessary to endure some temporary discomfort and pain in order to avoid much more serious suffering — and possibly even death — later on.

In that case, although our doctor is making us go through some rather unpleasant and distasteful procedures for a while, he is not out to harm us but to do us good. If we are wise, we will cooperate with his attempts to make us well and whole again, even if we don't like them.

That's how we need to look upon the work of the Great Physician. We need to learn to appreciate His efforts on our behalf and to cooperate with Him — even though for the moment it may not be very exciting or enjoyable.

It Hurts Good!

For the time being no discipline brings joy, but seems grievous and painful; but afterwards it

*yields a peaceable fruit of righteousness to
those who have been trained by it [a harvest of
fruit which consists in righteousness — in
conformity to God's will in purpose, thought,
and action, resulting in right living and right
standing with God].*
*So then, brace up and reinvigorate and set
right your slackened and weakened and
drooping hands and strengthen your feeble
and palsied and tottering knees.*

Hebrews 12:11,12

When the Lord tells us that His ways
are not our ways, we have some capacity
to understand what He means. We are
usually able to recognize and admit that
we are not nearly as knowing and loving
and caring as God is.

But in that same passage God also
tells us that His thoughts are not our

thoughts. Often what He is talking about is our attitude.

Many times it is much harder and much more painful to change our attitude than it is to change our actions.

I don't know about you, but initially when God begins to deal with me about my attitude, I really don't want to hear what He has to say. Usually I try to ignore it. I try not to listen. Why? Because it is so painful to have to admit I am wrong and need to change.

One of my greatest faults has been stubbornness, pride, and hardheadedness. For many reasons, going all the way back to my childhood, I tended to be oversensitive, overbearing, manipulative, controlling, demanding, and generally hard to live with. Although God is changing me, and I believe the "old man" I once was is dead — it seems that he occasionally comes back to haunt me.

Sometimes God has to give me a dose of my own medicine to teach me what it feels like to others when I treat them in wrong and hurtful ways. By Him allowing someone to treat me the way I've treated others at times, I learn a lesson.

That hurts. But it hurts good. By that I mean it does me good even though it is painful to my ego and my pride.

Sometimes pain must be inflicted upon us for our own good. That is called "suffering unto perfection." It is not a suffering that creates pain for the sake of revenge or even punishment. It is a

suffering that sets us free from pain —
the pain that we cause others, ourselves
and God Himself.

That's why we need to be alert and
attentive when God starts dealing with
us about our attitude and actions.
His purpose is not to harm us, but to do
us good — to bless us so we will be a
blessing to others.

Waiting Is an Attitude

But if we hope for what is still unseen by us,
we wait for it with patience and composure.
Romans 8:25

Waiting is an attitude, a positive inner
heart attitude that each of us needs to
develop.

We need to be less independent and more dependent upon the Lord. We need to learn to wait upon Him and look to Him for the strength, wisdom, courage, energy, and power necessary to live the kind of life to which He has called us and anointed us.

Until we learn it is waiting on the Lord that causes the anointing to increase and flow, we are going to continue to be weary warriors and fainting saints.

*God Resists the Proud and
Exalts the Humble — in Due Time*

...God sets Himself against the proud and haughty, but gives grace [continually] to the lowly (those who are humble enough to receive it)....
Humble yourselves [feeling very

insignificant] in the presence of the Lord, and
He will exalt you [He will lift you up and
make your lives significant].

James 4:6,10

According to James, if we will humble ourselves God will exalt us and lift us up and make our lives significant. But if we are proud and haughty God Himself will block the flow of His divine energy from coming to us until we learn it is the humble person who receives help from Him.

Peter tells us the same thing, that ...*God sets Himself against the proud (the insolent, the overbearing, the disdainful, the presumptuous, the boastful) — and He opposes, frustrates, and defeats them], but gives grace (favor, blessing) to the humble* (1 Peter 5:5).

Then he goes on to warn us, *Therefore humble yourselves [demote, lower yourselves in your own estimation] under the mighty hand of God, that in due time He may exalt you* (v. 6).

In His Word God has promised to resist the proud and to exalt the humble, but in due time. That's why we must develop patience and the ability to wait on the Lord.

Satan Exhausts But God Exalts

Years ago before I learned this lesson, I was wearing myself out. I was trying to change myself, perfect my family, and make my ministry grow. I was trying to prosper financially and be healed physically and emotionally, and do all the other good works I thought I ought to be doing as a Christian and a minister of the Gospel.

As a result I was a weary warrior and a fainting saint. I was going around constantly complaining to the Lord, saying, "O God, I am so tired of all this. I just can't do it any more" — as though God had told me to do it in the first place!

Then one day I heard someone say something that really struck me. He said, "God is not impressed with your tiredness."

Sometimes we go around telling God how tired we are as though that is really going to impress Him. But the Lord never asked us to wear ourselves out. He asked us to abide in Him so we can bear much fruit, but also so we can run and not get weary and walk and not faint.

That is not to say that we will never get fatigued. But it does mean that we are not to drag ourselves through life physically exhausted, mentally burned out, emotionally drained, and spiritually frustrated from trying to do a bunch of religious works God has never chosen or anointed us to do. If we do that, we are not going to present a very attractive picture of the Gospel to the world around us.

God wants to exalt us, but Satan wants to exhaust us. That's why we must be on our guard against becoming so works-oriented.

Instead of wearing ourselves out trying to do all kinds of good works, we need to learn to surrender ourselves to the Lord and let Him do them through us.

We need to come to the place where we abandon ourselves and our situation entirely to God, asking Him to take over and work out in us and through us what needs to be done in our life.

As I mentioned earlier in the book, one time I was so worn out from all my struggling and striving, I found myself down on the floor on my knees very dramatically crying out to God. I was weeping and wailing and saying to the Lord, "Nobody loves me or appreciates me. Nobody cares what happens to me. I am trying so hard, and it's all for nothing. I just don't think I can go on like this any more. I quit! I give up!"

When I said that, the Lord finally spoke up and said, "Really?"

From that experience God taught me that the only time He gets to do anything for us is when we quit, when we give up our own works long enough for Him to go to work for us.

When we finally get through letting Satan exhaust us, then we are ready to start letting God exalt us.

Give It Up!

Unto You, O Lord, do I bring my life.
Psalm 25:1

I love this verse because it gives us the answer to our whole life: give it to the Lord.

We need to start each day with that affirmation: "Unto You, O Lord, do I bring my life."

That doesn't mean just bringing Him our worries and our problems. It means bringing Him our entire existence and everything it entails. If we will get hold of that truth, it will set us free from weariness and fainting in every aspect of our life.

I used to get so worn out trying to prepare for my meetings. I would go around praying in the Holy Spirit, trying to build myself up. I would work so hard at being "spiritual" I would forget to eat or sleep or hardly even breathe. I was getting myself all pumped up for what I was going to do for God. I was afraid to relax — I felt I had to be intense about the whole thing.

Do you know what I have learned? I don't have to do all that to be ready to minister in the name of the Lord. All I have to do is just abide in Him and do what He leads me to do. He leads me to be prepared but not to be exhausted.

Now when I am ministering to others I can relax and take things in stride, just as I do in my everyday life.

It is such a relief not to have to try to be "super-spiritual" all the time. Now I can just be myself, knowing that as long as I abide in the Lord He will abide in me and do His work through me.

I don't need God just when I have to get up in front of an audience and minister; I need Him all the time, for everything. I need Him just to get up out of the bed in the morning and to make it through my day. That's why I spend time

in His presence, waiting on Him.
Because when I do that, He provides me
with whatever I may be lacking.

Like Paul I have learned to glory in my
weaknesses, knowing that it is through
them that God reveals His strength. (2
Corinthians 12:9.)

God will continue to keep us strong
as long as we continue to wait on Him,
spend time with Him, and remain
dependent upon Him.

Trust in God With All Your
Heart and Then Do Your Part

O my God, I trust, lean on, rely on, and am
confident in You. Let me not be put to shame
or [my hope in You] be disappointed; let not
my enemies triumph over me.

*Yes, let none who trust and wait hopefully and
look for You be put to shame or be
disappointed; let them be ashamed who forsake
the right or deal treacherously without cause.
Show me Your ways, O Lord; teach me
Your paths.
Guide me in Your truth and faithfulness and
teach me, for You are the God of my salvation;
for You [You only and altogether] do I wait
[expectantly] all the day long.*

Psalm 25:2-5

When the Bible speaks of waiting on the Lord, it is not talking about sitting in a chair all day doing nothing. It is talking about having an inner-heart attitude of reliance and dependence on God while we are going about our everyday activities of life.

Yes, you and I are to believe in God and put our faith in Him to act on our behalf. But we must also put forth a certain amount of effort on our own behalf.

If we are going to avoid becoming weary and faint, then we must learn how God deals with us and what He expects from us.

We must learn how God *operates* so we can learn how to *cooperate*.

And one way we cooperate is by being encouraged in the Lord.

9

BE ENCOURAGED

So David and his men came to the town, and
behold, it was burned, and their wives and
sons and daughters were taken captive.
Then David and the men with him lifted up
their voices and wept until they had no more
strength to weep....
David was greatly distressed, for the men
spoke of stoning him because the souls of them
all were bitterly grieved, each man for his sons
and daughters. But David encouraged and
strengthened himself in the Lord his God.

1 Samuel 30:3,4,6

All of us need encouragement. We need
to encourage others, we need to be
encouraged by others, and we need to

encourage ourselves in the Lord, as David did in this passage.

This situation was really nothing new to David. All of his life he had to encourage and strengthen himself in the Lord.

As a young man facing Goliath all alone, David needed encouragement, but nobody gave it to him because they did not believe he had a chance of overcoming the giant.

In that situation, as in every hard circumstance of his life, David encouraged and strengthened himself by remembering how God had delivered him from the wild beasts while he was tending his father's sheep.

That's why he could be so bold and confident in the face of danger, as he told

King Saul: ...*The Lord Who delivered me out of the paw of the lion and out of the paw of the bear, He will deliver me out of the hand of this Philistine...* (1 Samuel 17:37).

That is what you and I should do when we are confronted with the giants of life, with problems and challenges that threaten to overwhelm and overpower us. Rather than becoming discouraged, depressed, and devastated, we should stand firm in faith, calling on the Lord to strengthen us and lead us through to victory. Cooperate with God by remembering things that will encourage you and build your faith.

We need to remember that God is on our side. He has not brought us this far to abandon us.

We do not have to go through life worn out or burned out, weary or faint. Instead, we can do as Paul tells us in Ephesians 6:10: we can be strong in the Lord, empowered through our union with Him; drawing our strength from Him, that strength which His boundless might provides.

The Strength of the Lord

In his commentary on Isaiah 40:29-31, Matthew Henry writes of the Lord: "...he upholds the whole creation, and governs all the creatures...therefore, no doubt, he has power to relieve his church, when it is brought ever so low...."[1]

That means if we will humble ourselves before God, He has the power to relieve us of every burden.

Henry goes on to say of the Lord, "He gives strength and power to his people, and helps them by enabling them to help themselves."[2]

We can help ourselves, but only when God helps us to do so. Otherwise, we can do nothing.

Without God's Help, We Have No Hope

Dwell in Me, and I will dwell in you. [Live in Me, and I will live in you.] Just as no branch can bear fruit of itself without abiding in (being vitally united to) the vine, neither can you bear fruit unless you abide in Me.
I am the Vine; you are the branches. Whoever lives in Me and I in him bears much (abundant) fruit. However, apart from Me [cut off from vital union with Me] you can do nothing.

John 15:4,5

The mistake we often make is trying to encourage and strengthen ourselves without doing it "in the Lord" as David did.

You and I can help ourselves, we can encourage and strengthen ourselves, but only in the power and might of the Lord. How do we receive that power and might? By abiding in the Lord and calling on His name.

One of the most spiritual prayers we can pray is simply, "God, help me!"

For a full year, I went around praying that prayer. All through the day I would cry out from the depths of my being, "God, You have got to help me!"

During that desperate time I think God was delivering me from a spirit of independence.

All of my life I had been independent, for two important reasons. First, I was born with an independent personality; second, in my early life I was abused, and I made a covenant with myself never to become dependent upon anyone. My reasoning was that if I was never dependent on anyone, then no one could ever hurt me.

As the Lord dealt with me about my independent spirit, I had to repent of it. The Lord was teaching me what I am sharing with you in this book about the importance of giving up personal striving, struggling, and controlling, and simply surrendering to Him and His grace and mercy.

Each one of us must learn what I had to learn — total faith, confidence, and reliance on God and not on self.

As Frail as Grass

...All flesh is as frail as grass....
Isaiah 40:6

Matthew Henry says of God, "He can help the weak.... He will help the willing, will help those who, in a humble dependence upon him, help themselves, and will do well for those who do their best.... the youths and the young men...are strong, but are apt to think themselves stronger than they are. And they shall faint and be weary, yea, they shall utterly fail in their services, in their conflicts, and under their burdens; they shall soon be made to see the folly of trusting to themselves."[3]

You and I dare not try to depend upon ourselves because without the presence and power of the Holy Spirit within us, we do not have the strength or the ability to overcome the enemy and his devices. That's why we must depend totally upon the Lord to help us.

Only a Puff of Smoke

...What is the nature of your life? You are [really] but a wisp of vapor (a puff of smoke, a mist) that is visible for a little while and then disappears [into thin air].

James 4:14

What is a wisp of vapor, a puff of smoke, a mist going to accomplish on its own?

Nothing.

Without God, what can you and I hope to accomplish?

Nothing.

That's one reason we don't do more in this life than we do. It's because we try to act on our own, or we ask the Lord to act for us and then try to take credit for what He does for us.

The Lord gives us a little bit and then waits to see how we handle it. If we remain humble and grateful, still acknowledging our total dependence on Him, then He can continue to bless us and promote us.

But the moment we begin to think we can do anything without Him, the Lord begins to cut us off and let us fall on our face until we learn to acknowledge Him as our Source.

"My Soul Waits for God"

*For God alone my soul waits in silence; from
Him comes my salvation.
He only is my Rock and my Salvation,
my Defense and my Fortress, I shall not be
greatly moved.*

Psalm 62:1,2

Do you know what it means to say, "My soul waits for the Lord"? It means to trust God totally and completely without trying to figure out either the past or the future.

You and I need to learn just to enjoy God where we are at the moment, right now. He has everything under control. He was in our past, He is in our present, and He will be in our future. In fact, He is already out ahead of us paving the way. All He wants us to do is to trust Him enough to follow after Him in simple faith and obedience.

Even though we may not see where we are headed or even feel His presence with us, we must keep on taking the steps that are set before us, encouraging and strengthening ourselves with the knowledge that God is working out everything for the best for us as we follow Him in childlike faith and confidence. That is what is meant by looking to the Lord.

Look to the Lord!

My soul, wait only upon God and silently submit to Him; for my hope and expectation are from Him.

He only is my Rock and my Salvation; He is my Defense and my Fortress, I shall not be moved....Trust in, lean on, rely on, and have confidence in Him at all times, you people; pour out your hearts before Him....

Psalm 62:5,6,8

Are you looking to the wrong source for your hope and expectation? Are you angry at other people because they are not giving you what you think you need and want? If so, learn to look to God as your Source.

If you need encouragement, then let the Lord encourage you. Trust in, lean on, and have confidence in Him at all times; pour out your heart before Him and let Him strengthen and empower, refresh and renew, help and encourage you so you can live free of weariness and fainting all the days of your life.

Prayer for a Personal Relationship with the Lord

—∿∿—

If you have never invited Jesus, the Prince of Peace, to be your Lord and Savior, I invite you to do so now. Pray the following prayer, and if you are really sincere about it, you will experience a new life in Christ.

Father,

You loved the world so much, You gave Your only begotten Son to die for our sins so that whoever believes in Him will not perish, but have eternal life.

Your Word says we are saved by grace through faith as a gift from You. There is nothing we can do to earn salvation.

I believe and confess with my mouth that Jesus Christ is Your Son, the Savior of the world. I believe He died on the cross for me and bore all of my sins, paying the price for them. I believe in my heart that You raised Jesus from the dead.

I ask You to forgive my sins. I confess Jesus as my Lord. According to Your Word, I am saved and will spend eternity with You! Thank You, Father. I am so grateful! In Jesus' name, amen.

See John 3:16; Ephesians 2:8,9; Romans 10:9,10; 1 Corinthians 15:3,4; 1 John 1:9; 4:14-16; 5:1,12,13.

ENDNOTES

—◦◦◦—

CHAPTER 1

[1] William Wilson, *Wilson's Old Testament Word Studies* (Peabody: Hendrickson Publisher, n.d.), s.v. "WEARY," #3.

[2] *Webster's New World College Dictionary*, 3d ed. (New York: Macmillan, 1996), s.v. "weary."

[3] *Webster's II New College Dictionary* (Boston/New York: Houghton Mifflin Company, 1995), s.v. "weary."

[4] W.E. Vine, Merrill F. Unger, William White Jr., *Vine's Complete Expository Dictionary of Old and New Testament Words* (Nashville: Thomas Nelson, Inc., 1984), "New Testament Section," p. 574, s.v. "SICK, SICKLY, SICKNESS," "A. Verbs," 2.

[5] Vine, p. 221, s.v. "FAINT."

[6] Vine, p. 222, s.v. "FAINTHEARTED."

CHAPTER 9

[1] *Matthew Henry's Commentary On the Whole Bible, Reference Library Edition*, 6 vols. (Old Tappan, New Jersey: Fleming H. Revell, n.d.) 4:219.

[2] Ibid.

[3] Ibid.

About the Author

———❧———

Joyce Meyer has been teaching the Word of God since 1976 and in full-time ministry since 1980. She is the bestselling author of more than fifty inspirational books, including *How to Hear from God, Knowing God Intimately*, and *Battlefield of the Mind*. She has also released thousands of teaching cassettes and a complete video library. Joyce's *Enjoying Everyday Life* radio and television programs are broadcast around the world, and she travels extensively conducting conferences. Joyce and her husband, Dave, are the parents of four grown children and make their home in St. Louis, Missouri.

To contact the author write:

Joyce Meyer Ministries
P.O. Box 655
Fenton, Missouri 63026
or call: (636) 349–0303
Internet Address: www.joycemeyer.org

*Please include your testimony or help
received from this book when you write.
Your prayer requests are welcome.*

To contact the author
in Canada, please write:
Joyce Meyer Ministries Canada, Inc.
Lambeth Box 1300
London, ON N6P 1T5
or call: (636) 349–0303

In Australia, please write:
Joyce Meyer Ministries Australia
Locked Bag 77
Mansfield Delivery Centre
Queensland 4122
or call: 07 3349 1200

In England, please write:
Joyce Meyer Ministries
P.O. Box 1549
Windsor
SL4 1GT
or call: (0) 1753–831102

Joyce Meyer Titles

Starting Your Day Right
Beauty for Ashes Revised Edition
How to Hear from God
Knowing God Intimately
The Power of Forgiveness
The Power of Determination
The Power of Being Positive
The Secrets of Spiritual Power
The Battle Belongs to the Lord
Secrets to Exceptional Living
Eight Ways to Keep the Devil Under Your Feet
Teenagers are People Too
Filled with the Spirit
Celebration of Simplicity
The Joy of Believing Prayer
Never Lose Heart
Being the Person God Made You to Be
A Leader in the Making
"Good Morning, This is God!" Gift Book
Jesus—Name Above All Names
"Good Morning, This is God!" Daily Calendar
Help Me—I'm Married!
Reduce Me to Love
Be Healed in Jesus' Name
How to Succeed at Being Yourself
Eat and Stay Thin
Weary Warriors, Fainting Saints
Life in the Word Journal
Life in the Word Devotional